Best Easy Day Hikes Series

Best Easy Day Hikes
Canyonlands and Arches

Second Edition

Bill Schneider

Published in cooperation with the National Park Service
and the Canyonlands Natural History Association

FALCONGUIDES ®

GUILFORD, CONNECTICUT
HELENA, MONTANA

AN IMPRINT OF THE GLOBE PEQUOT PRESS

FALCONGUIDES®

Maps created by Mapping Specialists, Ltd. © 2006 Morris Book Publishing, LLC

ISSN 1553-2232
ISBN 978-0-7627-2563-2

Manufactured in the United States of America
Second Edition/Second Printing

To buy books in quantity for corporate use or incentives, call **(800) 962–0973** or e-mail **premiums@GlobePequot.com**.

The author and The Globe Pequot Press assume no liability for accidents happening to, or injuries sustained by, readers who engage in the activities described in this book.

Contents

Overview Map

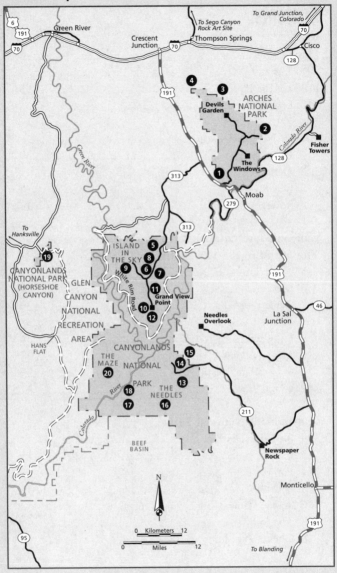

Canyonlands National Park:
The Maze District and Horseshoe Canyon 65

Introduction

While researching and writing a much larger book on Canyonlands and Arches called *Hiking Canyonlands and Arches National Parks,* I had frequent discussions with rangers on what kind of information hikers most requested. I also had the same discussions with many hikers out on the trails.

It seems that there are at least two general types of visitors —those who really want to spend several days experiencing the depth of the Canyonlands backcountry and those who have only a day or two and would like a choice sampling of the special features of the Canyonlands. This book is for the second group.

The more comprehensive book, *Hiking Canyonlands and Arches National Parks,* covers every trail and backcountry road in the two parks, including those that are neither best nor easy. This book includes only short, less strenuous hikes that are my recommendations for the nicest day hikes in these parks.

These hikes vary in length, but most are short. With the exception of the hike to the Great Gallery, none have seriously big hills. (The Great Gallery is such a great hike, that I decided to include it even though it has one steep hill). All hikes are on easy-to-follow trails with no off-trail sections. In some cases, however, it's not easy to get to the trailhead. You need a high-clearance four-wheel-drive vehicle to reach the trailheads for hikes to Angel Arch, the Joint Trail, Chesler Park Loop, and the Granary.

Some of the hikes in this book might not seem easy to some but will be easy to others. Please keep in mind that short does not always equal easy. Other factors such as elevation gain and trail conditions must be considered.

Type of Hikes

The suggested hikes in this book have been split into the following categories:

- **Loop:** Starts and finishes at the trailhead, with no (or very little) retracing of your steps.
- **Shuttle:** A point-to-point trip that requires two vehicles (one left at the other end of the trail) or a prearranged pick up at a designated time and place.
- **Out-and-back:** Requires traveling to a specific destination, then retracing your steps back to the trailhead.

Trail Contacts

Hikes 1, 2, 3, and 4: Arches National Park, P.O. Box 907, Moab, UT 84532; (435) 259–8161, www.nps.gov/arch.

Hikes 5, 6, 7, 8, 9, 10, 11, 12, 13, 14, 15, 16, 17, 18, 19, and 20: Canyonlands National Park, 2282 South West Resource Boulevard, Moab, UT 84532; (435) 719–2313; www.nps.gov/cany.

How to Use the Maps

The maps in this book that depict a detailed close-up of an area use elevation tints, called hypsometry, to portray relief. Each gray tone represents a range of equal elevation, as shown in the scale key with the map. These maps will give you a good idea of elevation gain and loss. The darker tones are lower elevations and the lighter grays are higher elevations. The lighter the tone, the higher the elevation. Narrow bands of different gray tones spaced closely together indicate steep terrain, whereas wider bands indicate areas of more gradual slope.

Zero Impact

Going into a national park such as Yellowstone is like visiting a famous museum. You obviously do not want to leave your mark on an art treasure in a museum. If everybody going through the museum left one little mark, the piece of art would be quickly destroyed—and of what value is a big building full of trashed art? The same goes for pristine wilderness such as Canyonlands and Arches National Parks, which are as magnificent as any masterpiece by any artist. If we all left just one little mark on the landscape, the wilderness would soon be despoiled.

A wilderness can accommodate lots of human use as long as everybody behaves. But a few thoughtless or uninformed visitors can ruin it for everybody who follows. The need for good manners applies to all wilderness users, not just backpackers. Day hikers should also strictly adhere to zero-impact principles. We all must leave no clues that we have gone before.

Three Falcon Zero Impact Principles

- Leave with everything you brought.
- Leave no sign of your visit.
- Leave the landscape as you found it.

Most of us know better than to litter. Be sure to leave nothing, regardless of how small it is, along the trail or at the campsite. This means you should pack out everything, including orange peels, can tops, cigarette butts, and gum wrappers. Also pick up any trash that others leave behind.

Follow the main trail. Avoid cutting switchbacks and walking on vegetation beside the trail. In the desert some terrain is very fragile, so if possible stay on the trail. If you're hiking off-trail, try to hike on slickrock or in canyon washes.

Don't pick up "souvenirs," such as rocks, antlers, or wild-flowers. The next person wants to see them, too, and collecting such souvenirs violates park regulations.

Avoid making loud noises that may disturb others. Remember, sound travels easily to the other side of the canyon. Be courteous.

Bury human waste 6 to 8 inches deep and pack out used toilet paper. This is a good reason to carry a lightweight trowel. Keep wastes at least 300 feet away from any water source.

Finally, and perhaps most important, strictly follow the golden rule of all hikers: If you pack it in, pack it out! Put your ear to the ground in the wilderness and listen carefully. Thousands of people coming behind you are thanking you for your courtesy and good sense.

Ranking the Hikes

The following list ranks the hikes in this book from easiest to hardest.

Easiest
- 14 Pothole Point
- 6 Mesa Arch
- 20 The Granary
- 1 Park Avenue
- 10 Murphy Point
- 13 Cave Spring
- 11 White Rim Overlook
- 12 Grand View
- 8 Whale Rock
- 9 Upheaval Dome Overlook
- 15 Slickrock Foot Trail
- 7 Aztec Butte
- 17 The Joint Trail
- 5 Neck Spring
- 2 Delicate Arch
- 4 Tower Arch
- 16 Squaw Canyon/Big Spring Canyon
- 3 Devils Garden
- 18 Chesler Park Loop
- 19 The Great Gallery

Hardest

Legend

Interstate	(70)	Campground	▲ (tent)
U.S. Highway	(191)	Campsite	▲
State Highway	(313)	Gate (Locked)	•—•
Interstate	═══	Mountain/Peak	▲
U.S. Highway	▬▬▬	Overlook/Viewpoint	◻
Other Paved Road	▬▬▬	Parking	🅿
Gravel Road	═══	Picnic	🏕
Unimproved Road	≡≡≡	Point of Interest	▪
Trail	- - - -	Ranger Station	▶
Highlighted Route	▬ ▬ ▬	Restroom	🚻
Shared Trail	- - - -	Spring	○⌐
Intermittent River/Lake	⌇⌇	Trailhead	🥾
River/Creek	∼	UTM Grid Tick	+
Lake/Large River	◗	Visitor Information	ℹ
Park Boundary	— - -		

Arches
National Park

Compared to many national parks, Arches is small (73,379 acres), but it's also very scenic and very popular. Moab, Utah, a small tourist hub just south of Arches, provides all services.

Arches was designated a national monument in 1929 and was then expanded and designated a national park in 1971. The park is open twenty-four hours a day, seven days a week, and the visitor center is open every day except Christmas from 8:00 A.M. to 4:30 P.M. from September to mid-April and later during summer months. The park has a fifty-two-site campground at Devils Garden, but places go on a first-come, first-served basis, and getting a spot can be difficult.

In Arches National Park, water, extreme temperatures, and other geologic forces have created the greatest diversity of arches in the world, along with many other multihued, finely sculpted rock formations. Delicate Arch, perhaps the park's most famous feature, shows up in an endless array of videos, postcards, posters, books, and magazines.

A hole in a rock has to have an opening of at least 3 feet to be officially listed as an arch and be given a name. Arches National Park has more than 2,400 arches, a preponderance of arches that makes Arches National Park unique. In fact, there is no place on earth even remotely like it.

Arches National Park is located 25 miles south of Interstate 70, or 5 miles north of Moab on U.S. Highway 191. The starting points for hikes are referenced from the entrance station.

1 Park Avenue

Start: Park Avenue Parking Area.
Type of hike: Shuttle.
Distance: 1 mile.

Maps: Trails Illustrated Arches
National Park and USGS Arches
National Park.

Finding the trailhead: The Park Avenue Parking Area is on your left
2.5 miles from the entrance station. The Courthouse Towers Parking
Area is on your right 3.7 miles from the entrance station, in the
shadow of massive Courthouse Towers.

The Hike

The Park Avenue Trail is most aptly named for New York
City's famous street. Early travelers noticed a similarity
between these sandstone spires and the humanmade skyscrapers, and the name stuck.

Although you can start at either end of this trail, starting
at the south end results in a downhill hike. If you want to
hike this trail as you leave the park, start at the north end and
have somebody pick you up at the south end. Then continue
out of the park. If you can't arrange a shuttle, this hike is definitely still worth taking, even with double the mileage (still
only 2 miles) by going out and back from either trailhead.

You'll really be missing something if you leave Arches
without taking this short hike. You can see the Courthouse
Towers, Tower of Babel, Three Gossips, Organ, and other
grand "skyscrapers" from the road, but if you don't take this
hike, you'll miss the truly stimulating experience of walking
among them.

Park Avenue

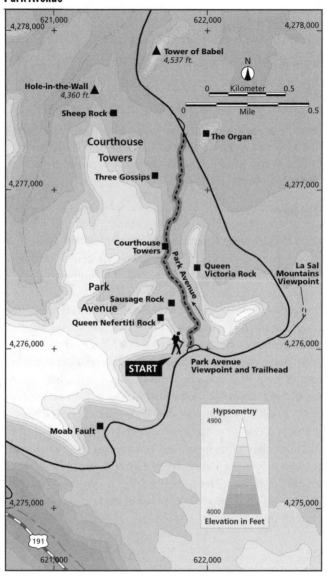

The trail starts out as a concrete path leading to a scenic overlook about 100 yards from the trailhead. From here a well-defined trail goes through juniper and cactus until it melts into a slickrock dry wash and stays there until just before you return to the main road. The trail disappears, but there's no chance of getting lost. Stay in the dry wash and follow well-placed cairns to the Courthouse Towers Parking Area.

2 Delicate Arch

Start: Wolfe Ranch Parking Area.
Type of hike: Out-and-back.
Distance: 3 miles.

Maps: Trails Illustrated Arches National Park and USGS Arches National Park.

Finding the trailhead: Drive 11.7 miles north into the park on the main road until you see the right-hand turn to Delicate Arch and Wolfe Ranch. Turn right and drive another 1.2 miles to the parking area on your left (north). Look to your right for a parking lot for oversize vehicles.

The Hike

If you've ever seen a postcard or poster of Arches National Park, you've probably seen Delicate Arch. This amazing arch has become the symbol of Arches National Park, which is somewhat surprising since it's barely visible from the road.

The trail to Delicate Arch is not a stroll. This is a real hike, and you should be prepared. Bring extra water (a minimum of one quart per person), wear good hiking shoes, and try to avoid the midday heat. The National Park Service (NPS) describes the trail as "moderately strenuous."

At the trailhead you can see the remains of the Wolfe

Delicate Arch

Delicate Arch ■

Delicate Arch Viewpoint ○

Delicate Arch Viewpoint Trail

Delicate Arch Trail

Winter Camp Wash

Cache Valley Wash

Salt Valley Wash

Salt Wash

START

Cache Valley Overlook ○

N

Kilometer

Mile

Hypsometry

Elevation in Feet

4900   4100

Ranch, settled in 1888 and abandoned in 1910. Shortly after leaving the trailhead, you cross over Salt Wash on a suspension bridge. Right after the suspension bridge, you might notice a large pile of "green stuff" on your right. This is volcanic ash that has a high iron content and has gone through a chemical process that gives it this greenish cast. Just after the bridge you can take a short side trip to the left to a Ute petroglyph panel. During the first part of the hike, watch for collared lizards. These large lizards can run on their hind feet when chasing prey.

For the first half mile or so, you hike on a wide, well-defined, mostly level trail. Then the excellent trail disappears, and you start a gradual ascent to Delicate Arch. Most of the rest of the trip is on slickrock, so be alert. You have to follow cairns the rest of the way, and sometimes the "cairns" are only one rock. As you get closer to Delicate Arch, you can see Frame Arch off to your right. This arch forms a perfect frame for a photograph of Delicate Arch. If you decide to climb up this short, steep slope to get that photograph, be careful.

Just before you get to Delicate Arch, the trail goes along a ledge for about 200 yards. This section of trail was blasted out of the cliff, and you can still see the bore holes in the rock. If you have children with you, watch them carefully in this section. Just after the ledge ends, you see Delicate Arch with its huge opening (33 feet wide and 45 feet high). You can take an awe-inspiring walk down to right below the arch, but you might ruin somebody's photo. A shot of Delicate Arch with the often snowcapped La Sal Mountains as a backdrop must be one of those photos every professional photographer has to have in his or her file, so one or two shutterbugs are usually setting up tripods for the grand view.

3 Devils Garden

Start: Devils Garden Trailhead Parking Area.
Type of hike: Out-and-back (to Landscape Arch) or loop (primitive loop).
Distance: 2 miles to Landscape Arch, 4 miles to Double O Arch, or 7.2 miles to Double O Arch returning by the Primitive Loop Trail, including all spur trails to points of interest.
Maps: Trails Illustrated Arches National Park and USGS Arches National Park.

Finding the trailhead: Drive north into the park on the main road for 19 miles and park in the large parking area at the Devils Garden Trailhead. The trailhead is at the end of the road where it makes a small loop. Be sure to stay on the loop instead of turning into the Devils Garden Campground.

The Hike

If you take the Primitive Loop and all of the short spur trails to nearby arches and other features, this becomes the longest hike on maintained trails in Arches National Park. It's also one of the most spectacular hikes you can take in any national park. However, taking the entire loop would probably not qualify as an easy hike, so you can make it an easy hike by merely turning back after seeing Landscape Arch and, perhaps, taking the short side trip to Pine Tree Arch.

Devils Garden

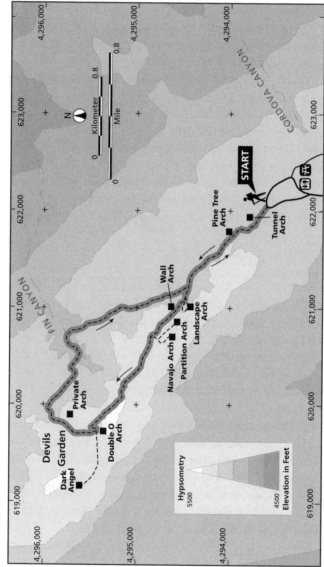

You can hike this entire loop in about two hours, but you could—and probably should—spend an entire day checking out the area and relaxing along the way. In any case, be sure to carry extra water. You might want to take this hike early to beat the heat and to be sure you find a parking spot in the large but heavily used parking area.

About a quarter mile from the trailhead, the trail splits. To go to Landscape Arch and Double O Arch and complete the loop, take the left-hand fork. The right-hand fork takes you on a short spur trail down to Pine Tree and Tunnel Arches. If you take this spur trail, it splits again at the bottom of a small hill. Go left to Pine Tree Arch and right to Tunnel Arch. After checking out these two large arches, head back to the main trail.

About a mile down the main trail, just before you see Landscape Arch and as you descend a series of steps, you see where the primitive loop trail comes in. You can take the loop either way, of course, but this description covers the clockwise route, so take a left at this junction and continue to Landscape Arch.

The hike to Landscape Arch (2 miles out-and-back) is akin to the trip to Delicate Arch. It's one of those must-see features of Arches National Park. This first part of the Devils Garden hike is a super trail—flat, easy, doublewide, and usually heavily populated with hikers. Landscape Arch has an opening spanning an incredible 306 feet, which may be the longest stone span in the world. On the geologic time scale, Landscape Arch is a senior citizen among arches in the park. The arch is also famous for the extreme slenderness of its stone span. Don't wait too long to see Landscape Arch. Geologically speaking it's likely to collapse any day.

Many people interested in a best easy hike turn back at Landscape Arch. Some hikers would not consider the rest of the Primitive Loop Trail an easy hike.

After Landscape Arch the trail gets less defined and stays that way. In fact, right after Landscape Arch the trail gets primitive for a short stretch, where it climbs over sandstone slabs and is marked with cairns. It's still easy to follow, though, and the trail all the way to Double O Arch gets lots of use. In this section you pass Wall Arch on your right. As at Landscape Arch you don't have to leave the main trail to see Wall Arch.

Another 0.25 mile up the trail, you see a short spur trail going off to the left to Partition and Navajo Arches. Partition Arch is the big arch you can see in the background when you're looking at Landscape Arch. Yes, Partition Arch has a partition, and the spur trail goes right up under the arch and ends—a great place to relax and soak in the view.

The trail to Navajo Arch also stops right under the arch—another great place for a break. This arch is shaded and perhaps an even better place than Partition Arch to stop and relax before continuing to Double O Arch.

When you get back on the main trail, it's another 0.5 mile to Double O Arch on a fairly rough trail that's mostly on slickrock and a little hard to follow. Double O Arch is most unusual, one arch on top of another. Just after Double O Arch, you hit a junction with a spur trail heading to the left to the Dark Angel. Taking this spur trail adds nearly a mile to your trip, but it's worth it to get a close look at this blackish sandstone spike jutting out of the desert landscape.

Also right after Double O Arch, the Primitive Loop Trail heads off to the right. The NPS has marked it CAUTION, PRIMITIVE TRAIL, DIFFICULT HIKING, and the loop section of this hike is about as difficult as the section between Landscape and Partition Arches, which you have already hiked. In winter some sections can be wet or icy, making footing quite slick. If you turn back at this point, you have seen most of the famous features of the Devils Garden Trail.

About half a mile up the Primitive Loop Trail, watch for a short spur trail going off to the right to Private Arch, the last arch you see on this loop. From here, instead of going from arch to arch like the first part of this trip, the loop trail traverses a beautiful desert environment where you can study the flora and fauna and probably have it all to yourself. Although thousands of hikers take the first part of this loop trip, most people choose to retrace their steps on a better trail than brave the Primitive Loop Trail route.

Miles and Directions

0.25 Spur trail to Tunnel and Pine Tree Arches.

0.8 Landscape Arch.

1.0 Wall Arch.

1.4 Navajo Arch, junction with Primitive Loop Trail, turn left.

1.5 Partition Arch.

2.0 Double O Arch.

2.1 Junction with Primitive Loop Trail, turn right.

2.5 Dark Angel.

2.9 Private Arch.

6.2 Junction with main trail, turn left.

7.2 Devils Garden Trailhead.

4 Tower Arch

Start: Tower Arch Trailhead.
Type of hike: Out-and-back.
Distance: 3.4 miles.

Maps: Trails Illustrated Arches
National Park and USGS Arches
National Park.

Finding the trailhead: Turn left (west) onto Salt Valley Road, which leaves the main road 16 miles beyond the entrance station. Follow the road for 7.1 miles until you see a junction with a sign pointing to a left turn to Klondike Bluffs. Take this road for 1.5 miles until it ends at the Tower Arch Trailhead. Be careful not to take the left turn (which leads to a difficult four-wheel-drive road) just before Klondike Bluffs Road.

The Hike

The trail to Tower Arch might stretch the definition of a best easy hike. But if you have the time and energy to take this hike, you will undoubtedly consider it time well spent.

The trail immediately starts to climb to the top of the bluff, up a steep but short incline. After this brief climb, the trail continues up and down until you see massive Tower Arch surrounded by a maze of spectacular sandstone spires. Along the way you get great views of the austere Klondike Bluffs on your right.

Part of the trail is on slickrock, so always be watching for the next cairn. The roughest part of the trail, however, goes through two stretches of loose sand near the end of the hike that make hiking uphill difficult. It's easy coming back, though.

Tower Arch

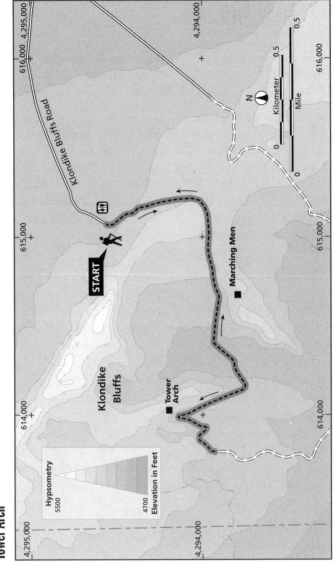

Klondike Bluffs Road

START

Klondike Bluffs

Tower Arch

Marching Men

Hypsometry
5500
4700
Elevation in Feet

N

Kilometer
0   0.5

Mile
0   0.5

You can climb up under the arch and get a great view while taking a deserved rest stop. In spring you see the magnificent, snowcapped La Sal Mountains to the east through the arch opening.

The return trip is noticeably easier than the way in. When you're at Tower Arch, you might see a vehicle just to the east. That's because you can drive around on a rough four-wheel-drive road, but those that do miss out on a great hike.

CANYONLANDS NATIONAL PARK:
The Island in the Sky District

The Island in the Sky District is a high-altitude mesa wedged between the Colorado and Green Rivers like a natural observation platform. The vistas here rival those found anywhere.

Although the trail system is not as extensive as in the Needles District, hikers can choose from a great variety of well-maintained trails. Trails dropping off the mesa and going to White Rim Road are for the serious hiker, but the area also has easy and moderate hiking opportunities.

Tourists with only a day or two to spend here can get some fantastic scenery from the main paved roads in the park, and the brief visit can be supplemented with several excellent short hikes on the mesa.

Rangers at the Island in the Sky Visitor Center (on your right about a mile past the entrance station) can answer your questions about the natural features and recreational opportunities found in the Island in the Sky District.

To reach the Island in the Sky District from Moab, drive north on U.S. Highway 191 10 miles to Highway 313. To reach the same point, drive 22 miles south from Interstate 70. Once on Highway 313, drive southwest 25 miles to the Island in the Sky Entrance Station.

5 Neck Spring

Start: Neck Spring Trailhead at Shafer Canyon Overlook.
Type of hike: Loop.
Distance: 5 miles.

Maps: Trails Illustrated Island in the Sky and USGS Musselman Arch.

Finding the trailhead: Drive 0.8 mile south of the Island in the Sky Visitor Center and turn left (east) into the Shafer Canyon Overlook Parking Area.

The Hike

This is one of the longest hikes in this book, but it's not difficult otherwise.

The Neck has historical significance. Here, the Island in the Sky plateau narrows to about 40 feet with sheer cliffs dropping off on both sides. This natural phenomenon allowed early ranchers who ran livestock in the area (before the park was created) to control the entire 43-square-mile mesa with one 40-foot fence across this narrow spot, later named the Neck.

Nature is also making a play at the Neck. Erosion is gradually wearing away the already narrow entrance to the Island in the Sky District. Sometime in the future, the Island in the Sky might really be an island.

One pleasant characteristic of the Neck Spring Trail is that it's a loop, one of the few in the Island in the Sky area. Most trails here are out-and-back or shuttles from road to road. This description follows the counterclockwise route. For more information you can get a small brochure about the Neck Spring area at the visitor center.

Neck Spring

Island in the Sky Visitor Center

START
Shafer Canyon Overlook
Shafer Trail Road
The Neck
Neck Spring
Cabin Spring
Neck Spring Trail

Hypsometry

6200
4600
Elevation in Feet

N

Kilometer
0   0.5
Mile
0   0.5

601,000   602,000   603,000   604,000

4,257,000

4,256,000

4,255,000

For hikers looking for an easy, half-day hike, this trail is ideal. The trail is well defined the entire way, with good footing (only one small slickrock section) and only minor elevation gain. Parts of the trail parallel the main road, but you're far enough away that you hardly notice. You do notice, however, the panoramic views from the trail.

The Neck Spring area allows hikers to experience a wide variety of high desert habitats in a small area. In spring the area often turns into a wildflower garden, so wildflower buffs will love this trail.

After leaving the trailhead, immediately cross the main road and continue on the trail on the other side. The first part of the trail is actually an old road built by ranchers who used Neck Spring as a water source. Along this section of trail, you see signs of past ranching activities, such as pipes and water troughs.

The trail then drops down in elevation and angles to the left toward Neck Spring, though not directly to the spring. However, you can easily see it. It's tempting to bushwhack over to the spring, but please enjoy it from a distance. This trail gets heavy use, and this is a very fragile area.

From the trail you notice a change in the vegetation with species such as Gambel oak and maidenhair fern able to exist in this area with its extra moisture and shade. Also watch for hummingbirds, deer, and other wild animals that frequent the area.

After Neck Spring the trail climbs slightly as you head toward the second major spring in the area, Cabin Spring. At the spring you see the same type of vegetation change as you did at Neck Spring—and a few aging signs of past ranching activity.

Shortly after Cabin Spring you face a short but steep climb up to the Island in the Sky mesa. The trail gets a little rough here, some of it on slickrock. When on top you get a grand vista of Upper Taylor Canyon and the Henry Mountains off in the distance. The last part of the trail follows the rim of the plateau directly above Cabin Spring and Neck Spring and through Gray's Pasture, a grassy bench used for cattle grazing until 1975. With no livestock grazing, the area's native grasses have begun to recover and now provide food for native species only.

After passing by the top of Neck Spring, you cross the main road again and follow the old road cut about half a mile back to the parking area. Be careful crossing and walking along the road.

6 Mesa Arch

Start: Mesa Arch Trailhead.
Type of hike: Loop.
Distance: 0.5 mile.

Maps: Trails Illustrated Island in the Sky and USGS Musselman Arch.

Finding the trailhead: Drive 6.3 miles south of the Island in the Sky Visitor Center and turn left (east) into the Mesa Arch Parking Area.

The Hike

This is a perfect trail for beginners. It's easy and short, and a detailed display at the trailhead explains how to hike the trail.

Even though the NPS manages this trail for beginners, it has something for everybody. Signs identify key plant species along the way, and at the end of the short loop, you are treated to spectacular Mesa Arch. The arch is right on the edge of a 500-foot cliff, part of a 1,200-foot drop into Buck Canyon. You can get a keyhole view of White Rim Country through the arch. If you walk back a few steps, you can also frame the lofty La Sal Mountains (usually snow topped in spring) with the arch.

The trail is well marked and partly on slickrock. It's an easy hike, but if you have children along, carefully watch them around the arch. There is no fence to prevent a sure-to-be-fatal fall. Also, please don't climb on the arch.

If you look carefully you can also see another arch from Mesa Arch Overlook—Washer Woman Arch—off to the left as you face the arch.

Mesa Arch

START

To 313

Island
in the
Sky

Mesa
Arch

Muffin
Butte

Aztec
Butte

Willow Seep

Green River
Overlook

Willow
Flat

Wilhite Trail

Kilometer

Mile

N

Hypsometry

6400

4000

Elevation in Feet

7 Aztec Butte

Start: Aztec Butte Trailhead.
Type of hike: Out-and-back.
Distance: 1.5 miles.

Maps: Trails Illustrated Island in the Sky and USGS Musselman Arch and Upheaval Dome.

Finding the trailhead: Drive 6.5 miles south of the Island in the Sky Visitor Center, turn right (west) at Upheaval Dome Road, go another 0.8 mile, and turn right (north) into the Aztec Butte Parking Area.

The Hike

This hike can be deceptively difficult. The first two-thirds of the trail are well defined and on packed sand. Near the end of the hike, however, you follow cairns as you climb about 200 feet up a difficult slickrock slope. Make sure you have appropriate shoes and be careful.

The climb up the slickrock slope to the top of the butte is more difficult than ascending Whale Rock (see Hike 8), and there are no handrails.

Once on top, you can see an ancient cliff dwelling called a granary. (Please look but don't touch, and resist entering the ruins.) You can also enjoy some great vistas, particularly the view toward the headwaters of massive Trail Canyon to the northwest.

Option: On the way back you can climb up and around the top of a similar butte between Aztec Butte and the trailhead. The hike is similar to the one of Aztec Butte, but shorter and

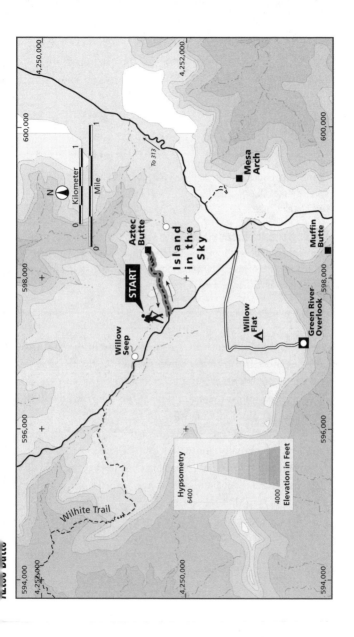

Aztec Butte

START

Island + in the Sky

To 313

Willow Seep

Willow Flat

Green River Overlook

Mesa Arch

Muffin Butte

Wilhite Trail

Hypsometry

6400

4000

Elevation in Feet

N

Kilometer

0   1

Mile

0   1

easier. If you want to take this option, watch for a trail veering off to the west just before you start going around the other, unnamed butte.

8 Whale Rock

Start: Whale Rock Trailhead.
Type of hike: Out-and-back.
Distance: 1 mile.

Maps: Trails Illustrated Island in the Sky and USGS Upheaval Dome

Finding the trailhead: Drive 6.5 miles south of the Island in the Sky Visitor Center and turn right (west) onto Upheaval Dome Road. Go another 3.9 miles to the Whale Rock Parking Area at the trailhead sign on the right (north) side of the road.

The Hike

If you want a great view of the entire Island in the Sky area, take the short climb to the top of Whale Rock. From there, you get a 360-degree panoramic look at the entire region. Plan on spending some extra time at the top to study all the interesting geologic formations.

The sign at the trailhead might say 0.25 mile to the overlook, but it's actually about 0.5 mile to the top. It's still an easy hike, though, and the NPS has made it even easier by installing five sets of handrails, bolted into the solid rock to help you get up the steepest spots.

The trail goes over slickrock most of the way, but it's carefully marked with cairns and handrails. Don't try to kick the cairns off the top of the rock—the NPS has used concrete to permanently affix them.

Whale Rock

Trail Canyon

Alcove Spring Trail

Syncline Loop Trail

Alcove Spring

Whale Rock

START

Buck Mesa

Syncline Valley

Dome

Syncline Backcountry Campsite

Syncline Zone (Backcountry Use Area)

Crater View Trail

Upheaval

Upheaval Canyon

Holeman Spring

Hypsometry

6200

4000

Elevation in Feet

N

Kilometer 1

Mile

0

And yes, if you use a little imagination, this rock outcrop sort of resembles a big old whale.

9 Upheaval Dome Overlook

Start: Upheaval Dome Parking Area.
Type of hike: Out-and-back.
Distance: 1 mile.

Maps: Trails Illustrated Island in the Sky and USGS Upheaval Dome.

Finding the trailhead: Drive 6.5 miles south of the Island in the Sky Visitor Center and turn right (west) on Upheaval Dome Road. Go another 4.8 miles to the Upheaval Dome Picnic Area at the end of the road. The trailhead is at the west end of the picnic area.

The Hike

This is a great way to observe and study the geological wonders of the Upheaval Dome area without taking the arduous 8-mile loop. In fact, you get a better view of the mysterious crater from this short trail.

About 100 yards up the trail from the parking lot, the loop trails break off to the left and right. Continue straight. The trail climbs the entire 0.5-mile distance to the first scenic viewpoint located on a slickrock outcrop. The NPS has provided an excellent interpretive display at the end of the trail that explains the geology of the area.

The trail continues on to a second slickrock viewpoint that gives you an even better look at the Upheaval Dome

Upheaval Dome Overlook

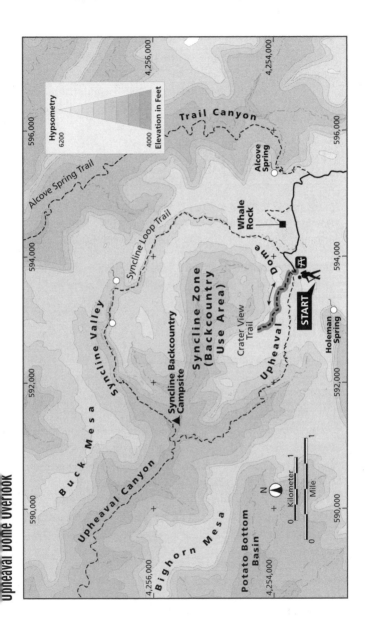

area. This increases the length of the trip to 2.5 miles, but the trip between the first and second overlook is only a gradual upgrade.

Both unfenced viewpoints drop off sharply on the west side, so be careful and keep children under close supervision.

10 **Murphy Point**

Start: Murphy Trailhead.
Type of hike: Out-and-back.
Distance: 4 miles.

Maps: Trails Illustrated Island in the Sky and USGS Monument Basin and Turks Head.

Finding the trailhead: Drive 8.6 miles south from the Island in the Sky Visitor Center and park at the pullout at the Murphy Trailhead.

The Hike

The Murphy Point Trail used to be Murphy Point Road, which went to within 0.2 mile of the overlook. In 1996 the NPS converted the road to a trail starting at the Murphy Trailhead. (Some older maps may still show it as a road.) This created a nice 2.5-mile hike with an absolutely stunning view.

This trail is mostly flat as it stays on the same level as the Island of the Sky. Because you walk on what used to be a two-wheel-drive road, it's easy going. About 0.2 mile from Murphy Point, the trail reaches the spot where vehicles used to park. The rest of the way is on an easy trail with some slickrock sections.

Murphy Point

START

To 313

Grand View Point

Buck Canyon Overlook

Murphy Point

Murphy Hogback Trail

Murphy Wash Trail

White Rim Road

N

Kilometer

Mile

Hypsometry

6100

4000

Elevation in Feet

From the point, you get a breathtaking view of White Rim Country west of the Island of the Sky, including the Green River slowly making its way to a grand meeting with the Colorado River a few miles later. Junction Butte dominates the southern horizon. You can see White Rim Road curving along the White Rim Sandstone far below. Plan on spending some extra time here relaxing and soaking in the incredible expansiveness of the Canyonlands.

You actually can spend the night on Murphy Point. The NPS has recently designated a backcountry campsite in the area. Ask about it at the visitor center. If a permit is available, you can park your vehicle at the Murphy Trailhead and hike about a mile into the Murphy Point area and spend the night.

11 White Rim Overlook

Start: Island in the Sky Picnic Area.
Type of hike: Out-and-back.
Distance: 1.5 miles.

Maps: Trails Illustrated Island in the Sky and USGS Monument Basin.

Finding the trailhead: Drive 11.2 miles south from the Island in the Sky Visitor Center and turn left (east) into the picnic area. There is no trailhead sign on the main road.

The Hike

You can get a good view of the White Rim area from the parking lot, but a short enjoyable walk gives you a really good view. The White Rim Overlook Trail starts at the right (south) side of the parking lot. It's flat and easy to follow the entire way. Some sections rely on well-placed cairns to show the way.

The trail ends at the end of a peninsula that juts out to the east from the Island in the Sky mesa. From the end of the trail, you can soak in an incredible panoramic view of the entire area. If it's near lunchtime, enjoy your lunch surrounded by the quiet beauty of the high desert before heading back to the parking lot.

11 White Rim Overlook; 12 Grand View

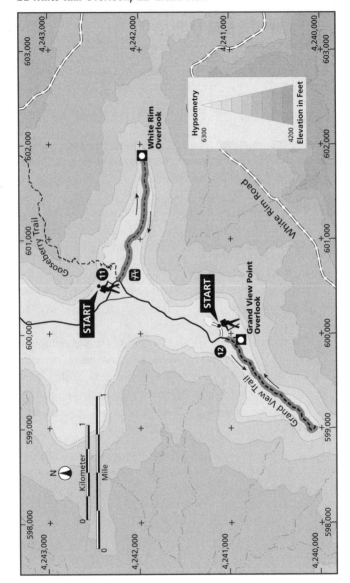

White Rim Overlook

Gooseberry Trail

White Rim Road

Grand View Point Overlook

Grand View Trail

START

START

Hypsometry

6300
4200
Elevation in Feet

N

Kilometer

Mile

0   1
0   1

12 Grand View

Start: Grand View Point Overlook.
Type of hike: Out-and-back.
Distance: 2 miles.

Maps: Trails Illustrated Island in the Sky and USGS Monument Basin.

Finding the trailhead: Drive south from the Island in the Sky Visitor Center for 12 miles all the way to the end of the main road.

The Hike

The NPS has placed several wonderful interpretive signs at the Grand View Trailhead, including a panoramic sign that names many of the prominent features in the area such as the Totem Pole (a 305-foot pillar formally called Standing Rock, the highest such feature in Monument Basin), the confluence of the Colorado and Green Rivers, and White Rim Road winding its way around the Island in the Sky.

The trail is relatively level with a few stairs at the beginning. Be careful not to get too close to the cliffs. It's a long way down. If you have small children, watch them carefully.

At the end of the trail, you can sit and absorb a grand view, contemplating how nature transformed what was formerly a featureless plain into what you see today.

CANYONLANDS NATIONAL PARK:
The Needles District

The Needles District of Canyonlands National Park is a high desert paradise—a jumbled landscape dominated by a series of distinctive sandstone spires called, of course, the Needles. Perhaps the other distinctive feature of the Needles District is an extensive trail system that offers nearly endless options for the hiker.

The Needles District has more hiking trails (about 55 miles) and a better variety of trails than the Island in the Sky or the Maze Districts. Plus, the area is, in general, set up and managed for hikers with lots of loop trails and a good selection of easy or moderate hiking options. Most trails do, however, have sections that go over slickrock, so you have to get used to following cairns.

The Needles District also has more water than other sections of Canyonlands or Arches National Parks. In spring you can often find a flowing stream in several canyons. (However, be sure to carry your own water instead of depending on unreliable desert water sources.) Also in spring, the entire area can be awash with wildflowers.

The Needles District has a great visitor center about a quarter mile past the entrance station. The Squaw Flat

Campground has twenty-six campsites with picnic tables, pit toilets, fire rings (bring your own wood), and a water supply (spring through fall). The campsites go on a first-come, first-served basis, and you'd be lucky to get one during peak seasons. The Needles District also has three group sites, which can be reserved in advance. Both individual sites in the campground and groups sites have nominal fees.

From Moab take U.S. Highway 191 south for 40 miles and turn right (west) onto Highway 211. Follow this paved road 35 miles to the Needles District Entrance Station. Be careful not to take Needles Overlook Road, which takes off a few miles before the correct junction. This road does not take you to Canyonlands National Park. Watch for the Canyonlands National Park sign before turning. From Monticello drive 14 miles north on US 191, and turn left (west) onto Highway 211.

13 Cave Spring

Start: Cave Spring Parking Area.
Type of hike: Loop.
Distance: 0.6 mile.

Maps: Trails Illustrated Needles
and USGS The Loop.

Finding the trailhead: Drive 0.9 mile west from the Needles
Entrance Station and take a left (south) onto a paved road (sign
points to Salt Creek). Go 0.5 mile before taking another left (east)
onto a dirt road. The unpaved road ends in 1.2 miles at the parking
area and trailhead for the Cave Spring Trail.

The Hike

If you're in the Needles area and have an extra hour, the
Cave Spring hike would be an easy and pleasant way to
spend it. The trailhead is conveniently located, and this short
hike offers lots of diversity. You can pick up a brochure that
explains the area's history and plant life at the trailhead.

This small loop trail goes by ruins of historic ranching
operations that were active here until 1975, when grazing
was abandoned in Canyonlands National Park. Please honor
the barriers put up by the NPS to preserve this part of the
area's history. Later the trail goes by Cave Spring and then
passes by some rock art left by the ancestral Pueblo Indians
who inhabited the area 1,000 years ago. Please don't touch
these rock-art treasures.

After you finish enjoying the signs of both recent and
ancient history, hike around a large "Canyonlands mush-
room" and climb a safety ladder to a slickrock flat. Here you
get the experience of following cairns over slickrock and
also get a great view of many of the area's main features such

Cave Spring

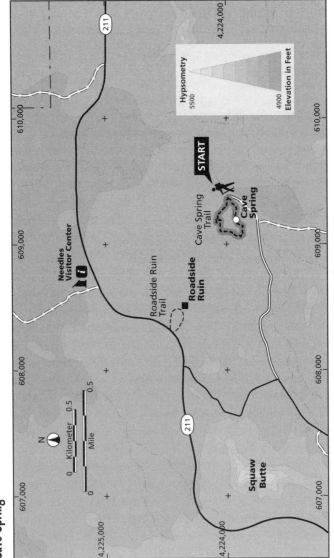

Hypsometry

5500

4900

Elevation in Feet

Needles Visitor Center

Roadside Ruin Trail

Roadside Ruin

Cave Spring Trail

START

Cave Spring

Squaw Butte

N

Kilometer

0   0.5

Mile

0   0.5

211

as the Needles, North Six-shooter Peak, and South Six-shooter Peak.

14 Pothole Point

Start: Pothole Point Parking Area.
Type of hike: Loop.
Distance: 0.6 mile.

Maps: Trails Illustrated Needles and USGS The Loop.

Finding the trailhead: From the Needles Entrance Station, drive 5.1 miles and park on the left (west) side of the road in the Pothole Point Parking Area.

The Hike

If you need a little exercise or want to take small children for an easy, safe hike where they might learn something about desert ecology, Pothole Point is an excellent choice. For a quarter you can buy a small brochure at the trailhead. The brochure explains the fascinating ecology of potholes.

Most of this hike follows a string of cairns over slickrock. The name "Pothole Point" comes from the numerous "potholes" that have formed in the slickrock along most of the trail. Once started, a pothole traps water after a desert rain. The rainwater is mildly acidic and ever so slowly enlarges the pothole. An intricate, symbiotic animal community featuring shrimp, worms, snails, and perhaps even a Great Basin spadefoot toad gradually develops in some potholes. If you're lucky enough to visit Pothole Point shortly after a rain, you can observe these tiny ecosystems.

Pothole Point

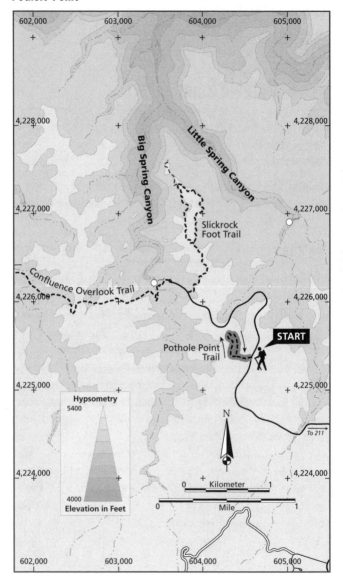

The wind continuously blows dirt, sand, and small bits of organic material into the potholes. Eventually plants take root in the thin layer of soil. The first life to appear is often cryptobiotic soil, which provides the foundation for the growth of larger plants. The end result is a "pothole garden," a pocket of miniature, bonsai-like vegetation in a bowl of solid rock.

You can hike this short loop in either direction. Watch for a spur trail going to the top of some big boulders where you can get a great view of the surrounding terrain in either direction, including the area's namesake, the Needles.

15 Slickrock Foot Trail

Start: Slickrock Foot Trail Parking Area.
Type of hike: Lollipop loop.

Distance: 2.4 miles.
Maps: Trails Illustrated Needles and USGS The Loop.

Finding the trailhead: From the Needles Entrance Station, drive 6.4 miles and park on the right (north) side of the road at the Slickrock Foot Trail Parking Area, just before the end of the road.

The Hike

If you're a beginning or experienced hiker with only half a day to spend in the Needles District, the Slickrock Foot Trail is an excellent way to enjoy it. Many hikes in the Needles follow canyon bottoms, but this trail stays high and gives an overall perspective of the entire southeastern corner of Canyonlands National Park.

Slickrock Foot Trail

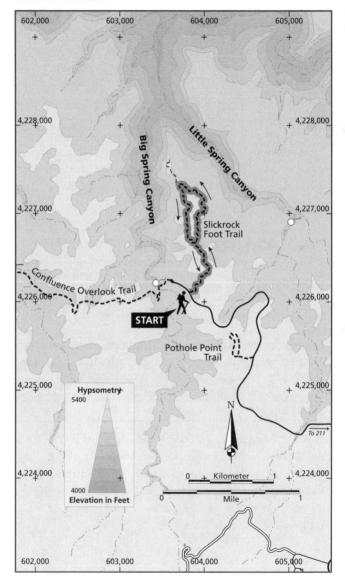

The NPS suggests this trail to inexperienced hikers so that they can get a look at the entire area before deciding where they want to go on their next trip. On this trail, beginners also learn how to follow cairns and hike on slickrock.

For the beginner who has only walked well-defined dirt trails, this hike might be a little adventuresome but certainly isn't dangerous. The trail is easy to follow with lots of cairns marking the way. Well-placed signs mark the way to four viewpoints and the point where the loop begins.

At the trailhead spend a quarter for a handy brochure written for this hike. It describes much of the geology of the area and is keyed specifically to four viewpoints along the trail.

Take this hike counterclockwise as indicated by an NPS sign about half a mile up the trail where the loop section of the trail begins. Viewpoint No. 1 is just before you get to the start of the loop. At this viewpoint you get a nice panoramic view of the entire region and many of the major landmarks—Six-shooter Peak, Elaterite Butte, Cathedral Butte, the La Sal Mountains, Ekker Butte, and of course, the Needles.

The trail stays on the ridge between Little Spring Canyon and Big Spring Canyon. At Viewpoint No. 2, you get a good view into the upper reaches of Little Spring Canyon.

After Viewpoint No. 3, the trail turns west and then south. You can take a long look at the region's namesake, the Needles, as you walk along.

Finding Viewpoint No. 4 is more difficult and time consuming than the first three. It's about a quarter-mile walk to this viewpoint, whereas the first three were only 50 to 100 feet off the trail.

At Viewpoint No. 4, you can look down into massive Big Spring Canyon. In spring you can see a live stream flowing in the distance far below. The brochure gives you a great geology lesson from this viewpoint, so plan on spending extra time here to identify all the different strata that make up the canyon's awesome cliffs.

After leaving Viewpoint No. 4, it's another mile or so back to the trailhead. Most of the trail follows the east flank of Big Spring Canyon.

16 Squaw Canyon/Big Spring Canyon

Start: Squaw Flat Trailhead.
Type of hike: Loop.
Distance: 7.5 miles.

Maps: Trails Illustrated Needles and USGS The Loop and Druid Arch.

Finding the trailhead: From the Needles Visitor Center, drive west for about 2.7 miles and turn left into Squaw Flat Campground. After entering the campground area, the road forks. Both forks go to trailheads with access to the same trails. However, the left-hand fork takes you to the trailhead with the shortest access route to the backcountry. Mostly campers staying in the campground use the right-hand fork and its respective trailhead.

The Hike

This is one of the most strenuous hikes in this book, and it might stretch the definition of *easy*. It's definitely one of the best hikes in Canyonlands, although it does require more physical ability and stamina than most other hikes in this book.

This might be the nicest, most accessible loop trail in all of Canyonlands National Park. It's nearly perfect for a moderate day hike to catch the essence of the Needles landscape, and since the NPS designated three backcountry campsites along this loop trail, it can also be an easy overnighter.

Squaw Canyon/Big Spring Canyon

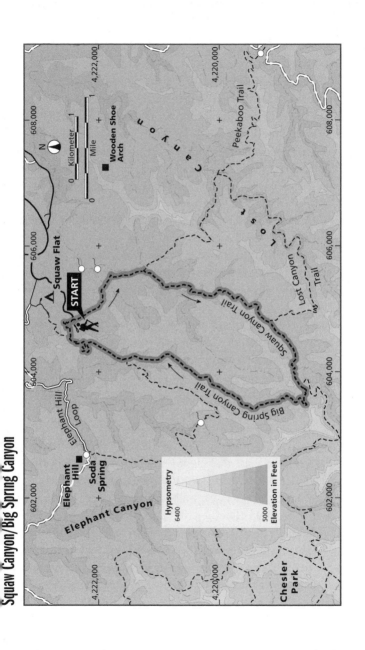

Immediately after leaving the trailhead, you hit the junction between Squaw Canyon and Big Spring Canyon Trails. You can take the loop either way; one way is not easier than the other. This description takes the clockwise route, because it makes two confusing spots in the trail easier to follow. Turn left (southeast) at this junction.

The next mile goes through fairly flat and open country (i.e., Squaw Flat) with scattered sections of slickrock. The slickrock sections aren't steep, but stay alert and follow small cairns showing the correct route.

When you reach the junction with the Peekaboo Trail, take a right (south) and head up Squaw Canyon. This leg of the loop trail follows Squaw Canyon, which often has a live stream in spring. Watch for Backcountry Campsite SQ1 on your right about a mile after the junction. If you're lucky enough to time your hike while the stream has water in it, you'll probably be treated to a course of spadefoot toad music. Please do not wade in the water.

The canyon narrows in places just before you hit the junction with the Lost Canyon Trail at the 2.8-mile mark. If you cross the wash, Backcountry Campsite SQ2 is down the trail about 100 yards on your left.

After this junction get prepared for walking over slickrock. After a short section of well-defined, sandy trail along the streambed, the trail climbs up on the north rim of the canyon and stays on slickrock all the way to the junction with the Big Spring Canyon Trail. This is a very scenic section and a good place to have lunch if you're on a day hike.

At the junction with the Big Spring Canyon Trail, go straight and follow a string of cairns as you climb up a short but steep section to the top of a slickrock pass where you get a great view of the surrounding landscape. After soaking in the scenery, climb back down to the bottom of Big Spring Canyon. Even though the NPS has expertly plotted the easiest route over this slickrock pass, this section can be hazardous, especially when wet or with children, so be careful.

After you get down into beautiful Big Spring Canyon, you might see some live water flowing, especially in spring. The canyon is narrow at this end but soon widens and stays that way until you get to the junction with the Chesler Park Trail. Backcountry Campsite BS2 is on your left about 1.5 miles down the canyon. BS1 is right at the junction with the Chesler Park Trail.

At this junction keep going straight (north) and head toward Squaw Flat Trailhead. Here the trail leaves Big Spring Canyon and heads across Squaw Flat. Just before you get to the trailhead, you see a trail going off to the left marked CAMPGROUND B. If you're staying at the campground, take a left. If you started at the main trailhead, take a right. From this junction it's only about a quarter-mile to the trailhead. The NPS has nicely routed the trail through some large boulders that in one spot look almost like a tunnel.

Miles and Directions

0.1   Junction with Squaw Canyon Trail, turn left.

1.1   Junction with Peekaboo Trail, turn right.

2.0   SQ1 Backcountry Campsite.

2.8   Junction with Lost Canyon Trail, turn right.

3.7   Junction with Big Spring Canyon Trail, turn right.

5.3   BS2 Backcountry Campsite.

6.3   Junction with Chesler Park Trail, turn right.

6.4   BS1 Backcountry Campsite.

7.5   Squaw Flat Trailhead.

17 The Joint Trail

Start: Chesler Park Trailhead.
Type of hike: Out-and-back.
Distance: 2 miles.

Maps: Trails Illustrated Needles and USGS Druid Arch.

Finding the trailhead: From the south park boundary take the four-wheel-drive road 4.7 miles into the park until you see the junction with the road to Chesler Park Trailhead. Turn right here and go 0.5 mile until the road dead-ends at the trailhead. The trailhead has a vault toilet and picnic tables.

The Hike

This is a most unusual hike. It's an excellent choice for those who want a little adventure (but not danger) and a hike that goes through some very interesting terrain (but not too long or too hard). The Joint Trail is just right for families with a four-wheel-drive vehicle. Getting to the trailhead is the hardest part of this trip.

This hike starts out uphill on a moderately rugged, rocky trail with cairns showing the way. In about half a mile, it dips into a long, narrow joint between two rock formations. From here it's like hiking in a very narrow slot canyon for about a quarter mile. A few spots require a handhold to scramble over rocks in the Joint, and near the end you climb some humanmade but rustic "stairs" just before you finally emerge from the depths of the Joint.

Just as you break out into daylight, you see a sign that indicates a short viewpoint trail heading right (south) from the junction. The Chesler Park Trail veers off to the left (east). The viewpoint is only about a quarter mile from the

The Joint Trail

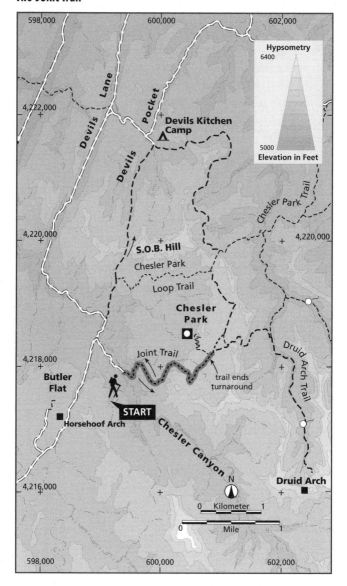

sign, but it involves a short climb onto a slickrock ledge. This might be a little nerve-racking for parents, but it's fairly safe. The steepest spots are made easier with little steps chipped out of the solid rock.

At the viewpoint you get a fantastic view of Chesler Park and its perimeter of stately, multihued sandstone formations including the Pinnacle to the north. After soaking in the view and having a pleasant rest and perhaps lunch, it's back into the "underground" of the Joint again on the way back to the trailhead.

18 Chesler Park Loop

Start: Chesler Park Trailhead.
Type of hike: Loop.
Distance: 5.8 miles.

Maps: Trails Illustrated Needles
and USGS Druid Arch.

Finding the trailhead: You need a high-clearance four-wheel-drive vehicle (and an experienced driver) to get to this trailhead. You have two options for getting there. The long scenic route starts at the Needles Entrance Station. From the station go 13 miles east on Highway 211 and turn right (south) onto Beef Basin/Elk Mountain Road. The sign at this junction parallels the road, so be careful not to miss it.

If you're coming from Moab or Monticello, turn onto Highway 211 and go 20.5 miles to the turnoff. From this junction, drive 42.8 miles to the park boundary. Unless it's wet, this road is suitable for two-wheel-drive vehicles. However, rain or snow can make it impassable. There are a few stretches of clay that get extremely greasy when wet, and this can make the road impassable for even four-wheel-drive vehicles. The rangers at the Needles Visitor Center keep close track of these road conditions. If there has been a recent rain, be sure to check with the NPS before heading up this road.

From the park boundary, take the four-wheel-drive road 4.7 miles into the park until you see the junction with the road to Chesler Park Trailhead. Turn right here and go 0.5 mile until the road dead-ends at the trailhead. The trailhead has a vault toilet and picnic tables.

You can also reach the Chesler Park Trailhead from the north from the Elephant Hill Trailhead. The first 1.5 miles of this road go over Elephant Hill, technical four-wheel driving most of the way. At the 1.5-mile mark, you see the one-way Cyclone Canyon Road joining, but you can't turn right here. Continue straight on this road, which angles south, and in 2 miles you come to the Devils Kitchen side road. Go west for 1 mile then south for another 3.1 miles until you cross Beef

Chesler Park Loop

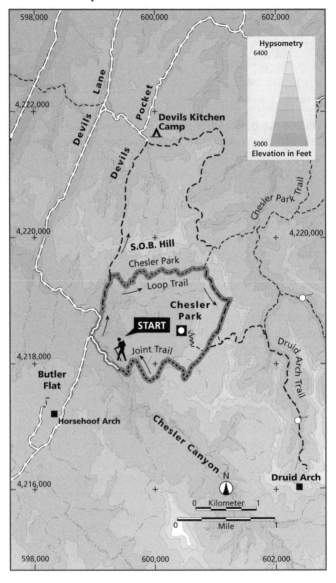

Hypsometry

6400

5000

Elevation in Feet

Basin Road. Again go straight, and in 0.5 mile you arrive at the Chesler Park Trailhead.

The Hike

If you like to save the best until last, take this trail clockwise. This involves walking on a road for the first 0.8 mile, but it's very easy going and you're unlikely to see any vehicles.

The road forks 0.5 mile after leaving the trailhead. The left fork goes south on Beef Basin Road. Take a right and walk another 0.3 mile until you see a sign for the Devils Pocket Trailhead. The sign for this trail is not right along the road, so watch for it a few feet up the trail.

The next section of trail involves a gradual climb up to a junction with the trail through the Pinnacle to Devils Kitchen Camp. Go right (east) at this junction and head for Chesler Park, which is 1.2 miles to the east.

You go through one rocky section with one short, steep pitch before coming out into gorgeous Chesler Park, a huge grassy flatland ringed by colorful sandstone spires. The trail goes along the north edge of the park for less than 0.5 mile before hitting the next junction.

At this junction turn right (south) toward the Joint Trail. Follow the east edge of Chesler Park on a nicely defined and packed dirt trail for 1.3 miles to the next junction. Just less than halfway through this section, you see Backcountry Campsite CP1 on your left. It's back from the trail about 100 yards, out of sight between several large boulders. This is a great choice if you're staying overnight. It's shady and more private than the four campsites 0.8 mile down the trail.

When you reach the junction with the Joint Trail, take a right (west). In less than 100 yards, you see a side trail to

Backcountry Campsites CP3, CP4, and CP5 off to your right and, a few steps down the trail, CP2 off to your left. CP2 and CP3 are fairly close to the trail; CP3 has the best view of Chesler Park. CP4 and CP5 are farther away from the main trail and more private.

All the campsites are tucked amid gigantic boulders where you can always find shade. You also see some signs of historic ranching operations, which took place in Chesler Park before the park was created.

From the campsites the trail is flat and easy walking. Long ago, parts of this trail were a primitive road. In 0.6 mile, you reach the start of the Joint and the side trail that goes to the right to the Chesler Park Overlook. Even though you've been walking through or on the edge of Chesler Park for a long time, you want to check out this viewpoint. It gives you a grand vista you don't get from the lower elevation trails. The viewpoint is only about a quarter mile off the main trail and well worth the little climb up to a slickrock platform. Here you get a better-than-postcard panoramic vista of Chesler Park and the sandstone formations surrounding it.

Back at the viewpoint sign, the trail dives into the Joint, a large crack between rock formations. As you climb down humanmade rock stairs to get to its depths, you might think you're not really on a trail, but you are. You stay in the Joint for another 0.25 mile. It's a tight squeeze in spots, but you shouldn't have any problems unless you're built like an NFL offensive lineman. However, you might have to push and twist to get a big backpack through the Joint.

After you come out into sunlight again, it's about half a mile on a fairly rocky trail down to the Chesler Park Trailhead where you started the loop hike.

Miles and Directions

0.5 Beef Basin Road junction, turn right.

0.8 Devils Pocket Trailhead.

1.6 Junction with Chesler Park Loop Trail, turn right.

2.8 Junction with Chesler Park Trail, turn right.

3.4 CP1 Backcountry Campsite.

4.1 Junction with Joint Trail, turn right.

4.2 CP2, CP3, CP4, and CP5 Backcountry Campsites.

4.8 Start of the Joint and Chesler Park Overlook junction, turn right.

5.3 End of the Joint.

5.8 Chesler Park Trailhead.

CANYONLANDS NATIONAL PARK:
The Maze District and Horseshoe Canyon

When you hear the old adage "in the middle of nowhere," they could easily be talking about the Maze District, and it would be a compliment. Most people have never been to a place as remote as the Maze.

Getting here is a great warmup for experiencing the Maze. Whether you come from Hite, Hanksville, or Green River, you definitely get the feeling of being out of touch with civilization long before you reach the park boundary. Then, when you start slowly maneuvering your vehicle up the primitive roads into the Maze, you complete the feeling of being totally self-reliant. The allure of extreme remoteness experienced in the Maze can't be found in most national parks.

Self-reliance is the undertone of the management policy of the Maze District. The network of twisted sandstone canyons is for rugged individuals who can take care of themselves and their vehicle. There's no gas station, restaurant food, or room service for 50-plus miles in any direction. And even 50 miles doesn't tell the true story, because it might take half a day to cover that distance on these roads.

In many national parks, including other sections of Canyonlands, the NPS provides great customer service. But not in the Maze. The Maze District of Canyonlands National Park combined with the Orange Cliffs Unit of Glen Canyon National Recreation Area is larger than many national parks, but once you leave the Hans Flat Ranger Station, there are no services, no guided tours, no facilities, no toilets, not even an entrance station. You are on your own.

Unless you wish to hike great distances, you can't fully experience the Maze without a high-clearance four-wheel-drive vehicle.

You can see small parts of the Maze District with a high-clearance, two-wheel-drive vehicle, but to see the best parts, you have to park it and hike long distances. A high-clearance four-wheel-drive vehicle is absolutely necessary to negotiate the difficult jeep trails in many sections of the Maze. A long wheelbase is problematic in a few spots, but you can usually get through them by backing up to make a tight corner.

The roads in the Maze can deteriorate rapidly when it rains and become treacherous regardless of what kind of vehicle you have. At the same time, fortunately, they dry out relatively fast. If you get caught in a big rain, it's best to wait a few hours for the roads to dry out.

After a heavy rain, the clay coating on some roads in the Maze (particularly the Flint Trail) makes them too slippery to drive. Also, in winter months ice and snow can make the roads impassable. During the winter the Flint Trail is usually closed.

Before you go to the Maze, make sure you know where you're going, what to bring, and how to prepare. This isn't like going to other national parks. If you show up without the necessary gear to survive on your own, you won't enjoy the Maze.

The staff at the Hans Flat Ranger Station is trained to help you and anxious to answer your questions on the phone. That's much better for both you and the NPS because it's much more difficult to deal with lack of preparation when you're already there. Call in advance of your visit at (435) 259–6513. If for some reason you can't get through on the Hans Flat phone system, call the park headquarters at (435) 259–7164. For reservations for vehicle campsites in the Maze, call the park reservation office at (435) 259–4351.

From Hanksville go north for 21 miles on Highway 24. Turn right (east) onto a major unpaved, two-wheel-drive road, which is marked with signs for the Glen Canyon National Recreation Area and Canyonlands National Park. From here it's 46 miles to Hans Flat Ranger Station, with right-hand turns at the 11-mile mark and the 24-mile mark. Both junctions are well signed.

From the Hite Marina on Lake Powell, take Highway 95 north 2 miles. Turn right (east) onto an unpaved two-wheel-drive road. From here it's about 59 miles to the Hans Flat Ranger Station, with several junctions once you get to the park, all well signed.

From Green River go to the middle of town and watch for Long Street. Turn south onto Long Street and follow it to the edge of town, following signs to the airport. The road stays paved until it passes under Interstate 70, and then it turns into an unpaved two-wheel-drive road. It stays that way for 68 miles to Hans Flat Ranger Station.

19 **The Great Gallery**

Start: West Rim Trailhead.
Type of hike: Out-and-back.
Distance: 6.5 miles.

Maps: Trails Illustrated Maze District/Northeast Glen Canyon and USGS Sugarloaf Butte.

Finding the trailhead: There are two ways to get to Horseshoe Canyon. You can take the hike down from the west rim (as described here) or you can drive into the canyon from the east. To get to the West Rim Trailhead, go 5 miles north of the junction between the Hanksville and Green River access roads to the Maze and watch for a small sign on the east side of the road that says HORSESHOE CANYON FOOT TRAIL 2 MILES. From here drive 2 miles on a two-wheel-drive road to the trailhead.

The Hike

This hike might stretch the definition of *easy,* but it's definitely one of the best hikes in Canyonlands National Park. It does, however, have a big hill to climb to get back out of the canyon, so be sure you're physically ready for it.

Although officially a "detached unit" of Canyonlands National Park, the Horseshoe Canyon area could be better described as a little hidden jewel lost in the desert. It's definitely worth the time it takes to get there. If you already plan on a few days in the Maze, you won't be disappointed if you spend half a day of your vacation at Horseshoe Canyon. If you're going to the Maze from Green River, Horseshoe Canyon is a convenient stop.

The Great Gallery is one of four major rock-art sites in Horseshoe Canyon, but the fabulous rock art is only part of the attraction. Horseshoe Canyon would be well worth the

The Great Gallery

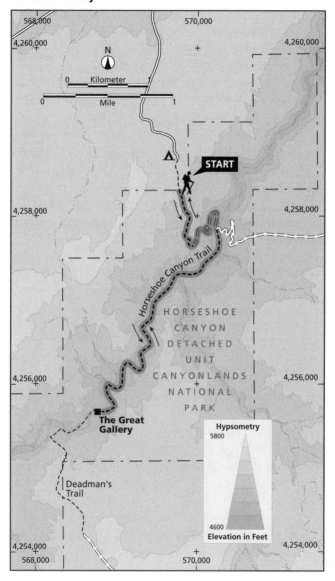

stop without it. It's a great day hike in a secluded canyon with majestic cottonwoods shading the sheer sandstone cliffs. The canyon has one other unusual trait: It's one of the few places in the Canyonlands with a fairly reliable water supply that is devoid of the evil tamarisk. NPS volunteers removed all the tammies a few years back, and now cottonwoods and other native vegetation are reclaiming the canyon.

Rangers lead a hike into the canyon at 9 A.M. on Saturday during the summer, but this is always subject to change. Call the Hans Flat Ranger Station, (435) 259–6513, to verify the schedule. If you have a large group but can't fit into the regular schedule, you may be able to arrange a special ranger-led tour. If you have a group of twenty or more people, you are required to have a ranger along.

You don't have to go with the ranger, but it's the best way to get a more complete story and history of Horseshoe Canyon. The ranger stops at each of the four rock-art sites to explain the history and prehistory and comment on the natural history of the hidden canyon along the way. If you want to get good photographs of the rock-art panels at the Great Gallery, early afternoon light is usually best.

The hike starts out on and then follows an old road from the west rim to the canyon floor. Since it's a road, the grade is not too steep. Nonetheless it drops 750 feet in elevation in about 1.5 miles, which can get the heart rate up on the way back. The road is mostly slickrock at the upper end and then turns to loose sand as you approach the canyon floor. This adds to the difficulty of climbing back out. Be sure to bring water.

On the way down you can see the remains of historic ranching operations (fences, pipes, water troughs, etc.). You can also see the austere four-wheel-drive road that drops into the canyon from the east rim. When you reach the canyon floor, the trail turns right and follows the canyon bottom for 1.75 miles to the Great Gallery.

A ranger often stays much of the day at the Great Gallery to answer questions. On the way into the Great Gallery, the first two rock-art panels have interpretive displays. Watch for short side trails. You don't want to miss any of them, but if you do you can catch them on the way back. Rock art is extremely fragile and extremely precious, so don't touch any of the figures or disturb any artifacts found in the canyon. These are irreplaceable treasures. Don't cross over the chain barriers placed around the rock art by the NPS.

The rock art in Horseshoe Canyon is considered a good example of the Barrier Canyon style, which dates back to the late Archaic period from 2,000 to 1,000 B.C. Later the ancestral Puebloans left their marks in the canyon, but apparently stayed only briefly. These early cultures were followed by modern cultures—cattle and sheep ranchers, oil prospectors, miners, and now, park visitors. Throughout all this use, however, the special character of the canyon has been wonderfully preserved. All visitors have the responsibility to do their part to keep it that way.

The Great Gallery is the last of four interpretive stops made by the ranger. It's a sprawling rock-art panel with large, intricate figures, both pictographs (painted figures) and petroglyphs (figures etched in the stone with a sharp object). When you reach the Great Gallery, stop for lunch, rest a while, and marvel at a few things. For example, even though the pictographs have faded slightly through the centuries, how did the early cultures come up with a paint that could last 3,000 years? What do the paintings really mean? What type of religious ceremonies might have occurred here? The ranger might toss out a few theories, and the NPS keeps some interpretive handouts at the Great Gallery, but nobody really knows what went on at the Great Gallery thirty centuries ago.

20 **The Granary**

Start: Trailhead just before turn to Dollhouse 1 Camp.
Type of hike: Loop.
Distance: 2 miles.

Maps: Trails Illustrated Maze District/Northeast Glen Canyon and USGS Spanish Bottom.

Finding the trailhead: You need a high-clearance four-wheel-drive vehicle (and an experienced driver) to make it to this trailhead. From Hans Flat Ranger Station, drive 2.5 miles to the Panorama Point junction and take a right (south) onto Gordon Flats Road. After 12.1 miles, turn left (east) and head down the Flint Trail switchbacks for 2.8 miles to Big Water Canyon Road, where you take a right (south). Follow this road along an exposed ledge and down a steep dugway for 3.5 miles to a four-way junction with Dollhouse Road. Turn left (northeast) and head for the Dollhouse and Land of Standing Rocks. Once on Dollhouse Road, stay on it for 20.8 miles until you reach the Dollhouse Camps. When you get to the Dollhouse area, the road forks. The right fork goes to the Dollhouse 3 Camp, and the left fork to Dollhouse 1 and Dollhouse 2. Take a left; the trailhead is about 50 feet after the trailhead going to the Confluence Overlook and 50 feet before you turn again to Dollhouse 1 Camp.

The Granary

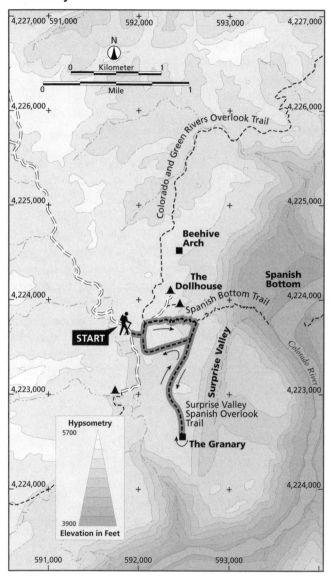

Hypsometry
5700

3900
Elevation in Feet

The Hike

The first part of this hike (which follows the same route as the Spanish Bottom Trail) is actually part of a small loop. After less than 0.5 mile of flat, easy hiking through the Dollhouse towers, you reach a junction. Take a right (west) here and head to the Granary instead of dropping off the edge of the plateau to Spanish Bottom.

After another 0.25 mile of easy walking, you reach yet another junction, with the Granary Trail going to the left. The right fork takes you back to the trailhead and you take it after you visit the Granary and see Surprise Valley.

Just before you reach the Granary, you see an overlook on your left only a few feet off the trail. From here you get a spectacular vista of Surprise Valley, a classic graben and a gorgeous one at that. About another 100 yards up the trail is the Granary, a typical storage place used by the ancestral Puebloans to hide grain for the lean winter months.

On the way back be sure to take the left fork at the first junction. This follows a well–laid out route through the Dollhouse, including a long stretch through joints in the sandstone formations. The entire trail is well defined, mostly packed dirt, and easy to follow.